Taking the Longing Out of Belonging

Kira Rosner

Artwork by Terrence Kennedy

COHERENT BOOKS

Taking the Longing Out of Belonging

First Edition

Copyright © 2011 Kira Rosner

Published by Coherent Books: www.KiraRosner.com

ISBN: 978-0-9679978-3-4
LCCN: 2009931485

Book and Cover Design by Kira Rosner
www.KiraRosner.com

Artwork © Terrence L. Kennedy
www.Higher-Essence.com

Printed and Distributed by Lightning Source, Inc.
www.LightningSource.com

Dedicated to four radiant stars. I am blessed to know each of you.

Julia Davis
Serenity Stone
Leilani Zimmerman
Kanoa Zimmerman

Gratitude

Samuel and Beatrice Rosner, Michael Rosner, Pianta, Jim Fairchild, Terrence and Linda Kennedy, Tim Shea, Jack Haas, Savitri Vidya, Gerri Scharf, Ronnie Newman, Connie and Jim Newton, Monte Walker, Rudy Wilson, Rodney and Nandini Charles, Bob and Judy Bernards, Paul Cohen, Tim and Michelle Campbell, John Giblin, June d'Estelle, Peter Navarro, Carole Glenn, Gail Stein, Girish and Asha Srivastava, Dawn Lianna, Oshara Helton, Winalee and Ron Zeeb, Denise Medved, Patti Gordon, Ghanshyan and Prem Gupta, Marilyn Carr, Jan Stevens, Harold Barlow, George Bresler, Ryan and Dana Love, Richard and Lynn Cassidy, Dharam and Hina Bhardwaj, Michael Albright, Beverly and Jay May, Mary Stevenson, Barry Whitfield, and all my beloved friends and family around the globe. I value your presence in my life.

Dear Readers

I love language and the playful way it shapes ideas. And I love sharing those ideas with people who are ready to embrace their inherent greatness.

This book is full of questions. Most are answered. Some are simply asked because I think stimulating self-discovery can be as beneficial as satisfying it.

Once we tap into our inner resources, we will see ourselves as the spiritual beings we truly are. We will always and forever be divine.

Table of Contents

Artwork © Terrence Kennedy

Artwork by Terrence Kennedy

1
The Seeker

Taking the Longing Out of Belonging

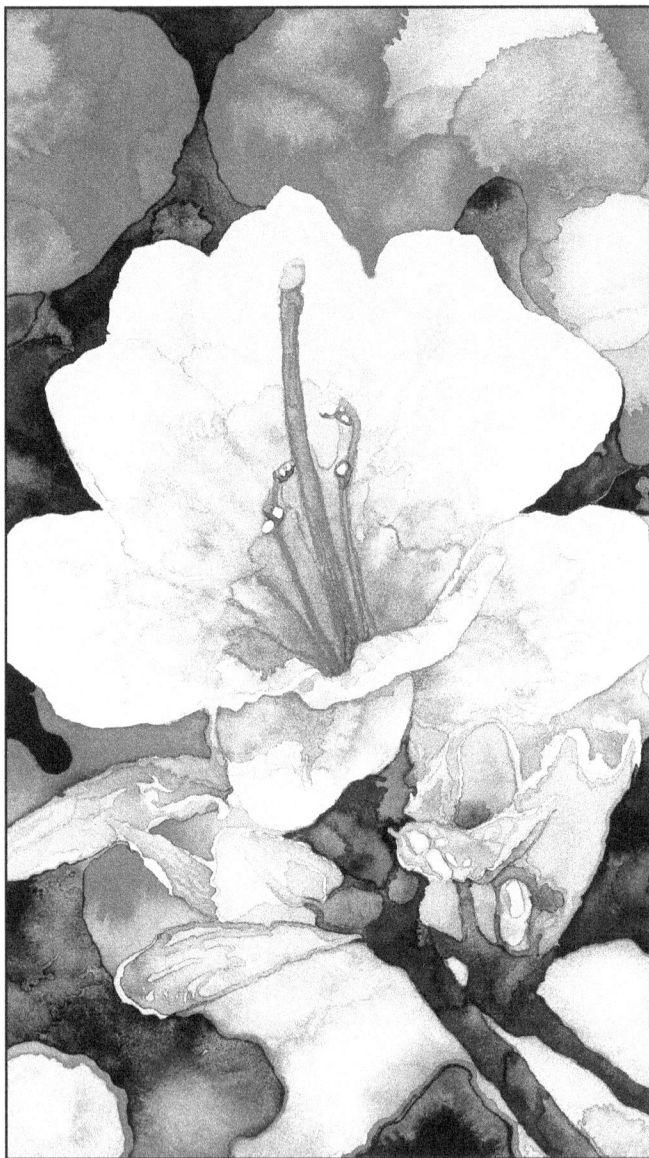

The Seeker

Like a fire blazing in the hearth, longing burns in me. "Reveal yourself," I cry, searching for something I cannot find because I don't even know what I am looking for. I only know an aching desire for relief that goes unanswered.

The only thing that keeps me going is the freedom dream I have each night:

> I am barefoot in a forest when time stops. I do not see, or hear, or taste, or smell, or feel anything. Suddenly, creation begins to breathe like a living organism and I feel everything.

> I am breathing too, only I'm no longer me. I am a watercolor version of myself engulfed in light, drawing energy from an endless source.

> Rapture fills me the same way music fills the air. No longer in the body or out, I'm everywhere at once.

Liberated by night, enslaved with longing by day, I try doing what others do. I study religion. Each one has merit, yet I still search for that which eludes me. I attend school and hear about those who have found their way. It only taunts me as I struggle to find mine.

Taking the Longing Out of Belonging

I move from place to place. In time, they all begin to feel the same. I work at different jobs. Their charm is temporary at best. I eat and my body swells. The hunger persists. I fast and feel lighter and more buoyant. My heart remains heavy.

I meet men. Their attention flatters me, entices me. The emptiness lingers, lurking around each corner like a cat stalking its prey.

The day I meet him, the relentless longing subsides. I lose myself in his emerald eyes.

2
Prophesy

Prophesy

L ose myself instead of find myself. I wonder, is this romance a homecoming or a diversion?

Guitar in hand, he drapes his lanky figure on a chair the color of crusty bread. Moments earlier, he had played me to the music of uncertainty, drawing us farther apart than closer together.

Apart, as our lips first parted, tenderly exploring the likelihood of a match, a fit, an answer to someday-ever-after. Flowering into an unspoken promise to try. Feel it out. See if it works. Give it a chance.

Moons later, we search for ourselves in one another. Our bodies intertwine in a symphony of illusions, while our spirits wait in the wings. In the morning light, the scent of peppermint tea and honey mask the emptiness I feel.

His laughter, his touch, the comfort of familiarity. It is almost enough to appease my longing to live without longing.

I have seen others who seem satisfied with almost. It's good enough for them, or is it?

When is enough enough?

Taking the Longing Out of Belonging

Prompted by visions that refuse pretense, questions circle my mind:

> What can we give to one another when our need to receive is as great as that which we offer?

> If I feel a void and my partner feels a void, do two voids cancel one another out? Or do they combine to form a bigger void twice the size?

> Is wholeness something we find in a relationship or bring to a relationship?

> If togetherness completes us, are we incomplete without it? Is sovereignty in partnership a dream-come-true or just a dream?

Watching him leave, it occurs to me. Whoever said it was fun while it lasted must have found a way to swallow bites of life, instead of letting them melt in your mouth and savoring the taste.

Molded like clay, shaped into believing the movies and the love songs. I'd seen and heard them all since I was old enough to listen and to yearn. There was always an image of a man who would find me (Was I lost?) and take me to a place called happiness.

Prophesy

Turning the pages of my life, I waited for my happy ending to begin. Is truth what it is or what it appears to be? Who planted my desires and watered them with billboards and commercials? Is reality a marketing campaign?

"Look past what you have been taught by others. Personalize your definitions."

Who said that? Whose voice is speaking inside my head? Is it my conscience, my intellect, my guide?

Do I even have a guide, or am I talking to myself? If I have a self to talk to, am I separate from it? Are two of us inhabiting the same body?

Either way, I like the suggestion. I know what to do. I will take the longing out of belonging, rekindling the memory of loving freely, when fear had more to do with hungry bears than hungry hearts – dispelling the myth that need equates with love.

Plus, I will update the dream. Instead of being swept off my feet, I prefer to be on them. Firmly rooted to the earth like a lilac bush exuding a sweetly scented fragrance, rousing memories of youth, forgotten but never lost.

And he, the one to share my sheet music. Will our hearts flow free of expectations? Two lovers sharing their bounty instead of seeking it. In power. In love. In harmony, the way instruments are in tune. Fulfilling the sacred prophesy that those who awaken walk in fullness, in grace, in matrimony with reverence.

3
Crossroads

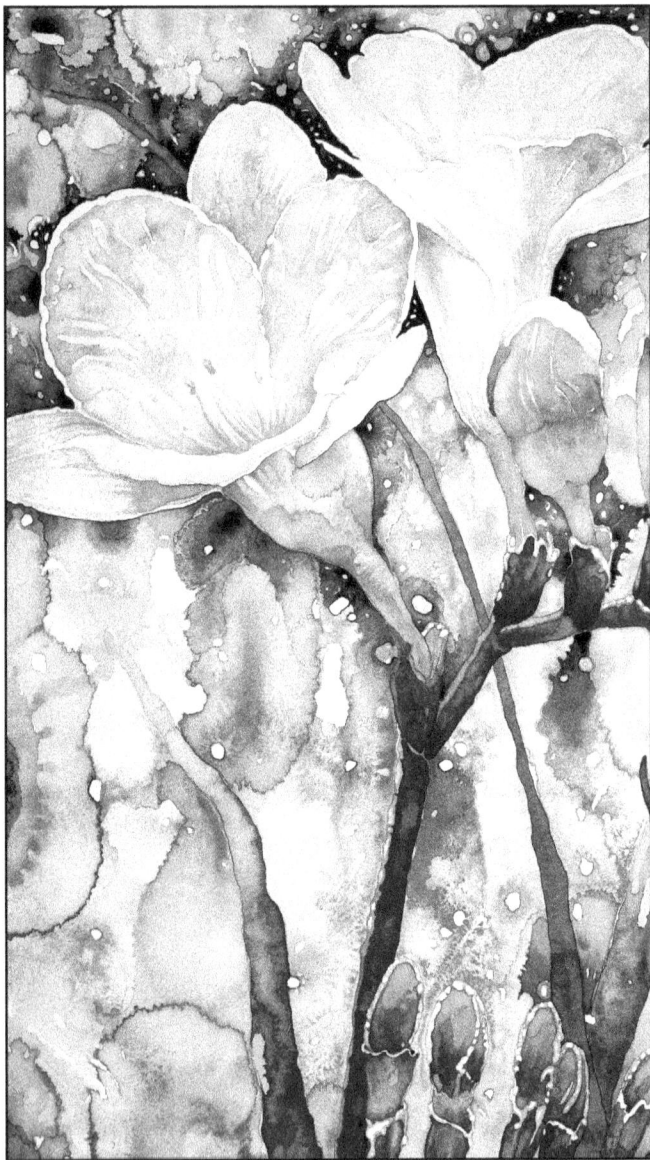

Crossroads

Have you heard? Science and spirituality are going out. Dating. Dancing cheek to cheek.

Perhaps, rather than lovers, they're study partners in the library with their heads buried in big books. One immersed in quantum physics, the other in ancient scriptures. Peering over each other's shoulders, they look for answers they expect to find in their own disciplines.

Instead, they discover a kinship. Like long lost siblings with the same parentage, they trace their family lineage to the crossroads, where the unknown laps at the shore of the known and science and spirituality meld. They commune, join hands.

Or more aptly, realize they were never divided. They only seemed to be going in different directions, while driving side-by-side down the information highway. One chauffeured by intellectual query, the other by passion. The difference is in the driver, not the destination.

Driven by a thirst for verifiable facts, science is after the impersonal truth. Driven by a thirst for revelations and divination, spirituality is after the personal truth.

But isn't truth truth? Isn't it whole and indivisible? No matter how we language it, isn't truth the universal elixir that harmonizes differences?

4
Self-Inquiry

Self-Inquiry

I recall sitting in a group of women. We had our eyes closed, quietly spiraling inward.

In the silence, I expanded. The walls couldn't contain me because I had no discernible beginning or end.

This morning something similar occurred. I awoke inside myself while the rest of me slept. Conscious within the confines of a body, I did not know I was confined. Momentarily, I was not sure where I was. Perhaps if you had been there, you could have told me that I had a self and I was awake inside it.

Do we all live inside ourselves? It is convenient, isn't it? A built-in retreat to retreat to when living on the outside gets hectic.

If each of us has a self we command, there are a lot of selves being commanded. Is there a bigger self, a commander who commands the commanders? Does part of the big Self occupy our small self?

Another thing. How do our minds know what they know? Are they like dictionaries written in the past to give meaning to the present? If so, our ability to interpret what's in front of us must rely on how we have interpreted what is behind us.

Taking the Longing Out of Belonging

That means, we have to remember what's behind us. To do that, we'd need a way to lock our memories in place so we don't forget what we remember.

Are beliefs memories locked into place?

(The voice. It's here again.)

"Beliefs are impressions from the past projected into the present," says the voice. "Experience waters the garden of your mind the way rain waters soil."

If beliefs are seeded by the past, that suggests they are learned. Many people consider their beliefs facts and hold on to them like mental banisters.

"Facts are impartial. Beliefs are personal," says the voice.

My problem is believing my life should be the way I believe it should be.

"Shoulds echo beliefs."

If shoulds echo beliefs, are yesterday's shoulds parenting me? Am I programmed by what I believe I should or shouldn't think, or feel, or say, or do?

Self-Inquiry

I have made a decision. I am going on a should-free diet! I will ask myself how I feel and take my cues from there.

"A cue is a signal or prompting."

Who is doing the prompting? Did my beliefs hire a director?

"It may help to think of your life as a book with the three main influences as the writers."

What three?

"Your Present Past, your Genetic Past, and your Soul Past."

Go on.

"Your 'Present Past' writes stories about your life experiences, basically what you learned growing up. Some of these lessons fostered your positive beliefs; others fostered your negative beliefs. Let's call this your Experiential Writer.

"Your 'Genetic Past' writes stories about traits that you inherited from your parents, who inherited them from previous generations in your family tree. These include attributes you are genetically predisposed to. We'll call this your Biological Writer.

"Your 'Soul Past' writes stories about past lives and from what it intends to learn in this life. Some call these stories your purpose or mission. Conceived before birth, they play a pivotal role in designing your life path. Call this your Inspired Writer.

"The person you are today represents a combination of your Present Past or life experience, your Genetic Past or heredity, your Soul Past or inspiration, and your powers."

What powers?

"As the editor of your life, you have the power to decide what goes to print."

5
Welcoming Magic

Welcoming Magic

If I have the power to decide what goes to print, where does my power get its power?

"Your power is encoded in your spiritual bond with spirit." (Aren't words fun?)

Where is spirit?

"There is no place it isn't."

What's the difference between people who consider themselves spiritual beings and those who don't?

"Mental concepts are formed by connecting ideas. People who identify with their spiritual nature have made a connection between the way they see themselves and the way they see spirituality."

Someone who doesn't, hasn't?

"Correct."

So individuals who are unaware of their divinity are as divine as those who are. The difference is in their awareness, not in them.

"That's true."

Taking the Longing Out of Belonging

When people are out of touch with their spirituality, they sometimes feel lost.

"An individual may feel lost, but it's far less likely to be lost. Because the human design is designed by the divine. Like a mobile trailer, your home goes with you. I do not mean the home you live in. I mean the home that lives in you."

How can I find the home that lives in me?

"Life is only hidden from those who hide from life. Chasing after what they want, they often fail to see what they have."

How can I see what I have?

"The surface values of life are constantly changing compared to the lasting stability which comes from communing within."

Are you suggesting I turn my attention inward to my thoughts and feelings?

"Thoughts and feelings are like ripples on the top of a pond. I am talking about communing with the pond itself."

Welcoming Magic

Please go on.

"There's a universal power that resides within you. Thinking, feeling, and acting are ways you express that power. But the real prize comes from contacting the power directly."

Do you mean tapping into the source of power?

"Yes."

When I do, will I enliven my divine essence?

"That essence is already lively. The only thing you lack (for lack of a better word) is knowledge of the part you play in the bigger picture."

How can I acquire this knowledge?

"By finding a qualified teacher who can instruct you in a meditation technique which effortlessly allows your mind to settle down until you transcend mental activity altogether."

Will my thoughts grow quieter and less distinct until they fall away entirely? Will I discover how freedom got its name?

"Meditation is a key to abundant wealth. It facilitates a process of refinement and purification, which is enhanced with every practice. The rewards are both immediate and cumulative."

What rewards?

"As a soul-based human, you have glorious presents waiting to be unwrapped. One of them is the ability to expand your vision."

Beyond what my mind and mirror tell me?

"Exactly. Right now, your perception is largely based on what you see around you. As plentiful as that is, it's only a partial view. When you transcend, that view opens like a window."

Physics speaks of a quantum field of energy that has no differentiating value. Will meditating allow me to experience this unified field, where life resides before it sprouts into being, before spirit becomes spiritual?

"When your mind quiets down in meditation, you'll begin to perceive finer and finer levels – to a plane of existence where energy resides in an undefined state of infinite creativity.

"Experiencing this unbounded awareness is blissful and life-changing. You will enjoy a deepening sense of wholeness and stability with each meditation."

Will I feel calmer and more relaxed? Will I begin to feel an inner happiness?

"Yes."

Will I gain an intimate understanding of the subtle dynamics of creation?

"Yes."

How will meditating help me change the world?

"Every thought you think, every feeling you feel, and every action you perform is an expression of energy, and energy vibrates. Those vibrations generate an influence. When you feel peaceful, that's the kind of influence you generate. When you feel anxious and fearful, that's the kind of influence you generate.

"Each man, woman and child is a thread in a global tapestry. Your contributions can strengthen the fabric or weaken it. When you meditate regularly, you strengthen it."

When more of us strengthen it than weaken it, will we have more solutions than problems?

"Naturally."

Please continue.

" It is analogous to pulling on a table leg. When you pull on the leg, the whole table moves because the leg is connected to the table. Humanity is connected energetically, so everyone's actions affect everyone else."

All this from directing my gaze inward?

"Directing your gaze inward opens the palace gates and offers you a direct link to wonder, and wonder is the stuff dreams are made of.

"Wonder connects your personality to your soul and your soul to your source. When you tune in to that mystical connection, the true fullness of wonder is revealed. Wonder-full welcomes magic."

I would like to welcome more magic, but how does one unravel the mysteries of the universe sitting with their eyes closed? It sounds remarkable.

Welcoming Magic

"Human beings are remarkable. You're an evolving, multi-dimensional race with the innate potential to realize your innate potential."

What is potential?

"Divinity's gift to humanity."

Can I really contact power at its source?

"When you transcend mental activity, you will meet divine forces face to face. This may sound abstract when you try to find words to explain it, but that is the beauty of being human. You are capable of experiencing a level of awareness where there are no words and there is no trying."

I still have so many questions.

"Reasoning and curiosity entertain the mind as you balance on the ledge of all things possible. Until that defining moment when moments no longer have definition and you find yourself immersed in the sweetest, lightest, ethereal sensation. A feeling that stays with you whether your eyes are closed or open, filling you with the same satisfying quality as a deep meditation."

Is that what enlightenment is?

"Enlightenment is a renewed innocence. An exalted state in which all thoughts of finding happiness are replaced by a knowingness, a certainty, that life is not what you take from it, but what you bring to it."

6
Perception

Perception

Eyelashes waving in the wind, I close my eyes and step inside myself. It's quiet in here and dark. Wait, I think I hear a thought. Isn't the thought that I hear a thought also a thought?

Where are thoughts before we think them? Do they line up on shelves like books in a library, waiting to get passed from one thinker to another – parents giving them to children who later become parents themselves? Are thoughts recycled? Look at that. A mind asking questions about itself.

What about those peaceful moments when thought is absent? Silence is present. Is silence ever absent or ever-present? Do thoughts personify silence? Does all of life?

Maybe thoughts are creative impulses, mental blips which give direction to that which has yet to take on direction. Formless until they are formed, thought-less until they are thought, existing in the field of readiness alone.

Amazing! From my private observation deck, I can see the landscape of the mind as it multi-tasks with extreme precision. A circus with more rings than I can count.

I see the five senses rushing back and forth, busily receiving input for the mind to digest. One second, they are out gathering data. In a flash, they are back reporting what they've seen, heard, tasted, touched, and smelled to the keeper of the past, who confers with our memory files to arrive at a context or interpretation.

There's more. Perception is not confirmed without our belief committee, who gives the final stamp of approval or disapproval. So what we see is not only what we see. It's what we believe we see.

Facinating! I see experience leaving impressions in our mental gardens. Some add to the large volumes of data already there. Others band together to form the beliefs which govern our decisions – when we let them.

I see the pool of plenty, home to the imagination. It is filled with colors swirling together, arranging and rearranging dreams as they are dreamt.

I see choice sitting on her regal throne, surveying the workings of the mind like an empress surveying her subjects. Intention waits nearby, ready to rush to the side of any purpose.

Perception

How curious. Choice has a cell phone at each ear and is conversing with the heart and body simultaneously. Apparently, the mind stays in close contact with both.

The soul, whose presence is sparkling, is attempting to speak through the heart in the hopes that someone is listening. Since it is my mind I am observing, I suppose that someone would be me.

Are you surprised that I can hear the soul speaking through the heart when I'm observing the mind? I am, too.

Look! There are senses emanating from the soul. It is feeling, and seeing, and hearing, and tasting, and smelling. We know our corporeal body has physical senses. It seems our spiritual body has metaphysical senses.

Meta means beyond. Metaphysical means beyond the physical. If our souls can sense beyond the physical – there must be something beyond the physical to sense!

Is that what seers do? Are they busy mining for gold while the rest of us are out jewelry shopping?

If perception is a by-product of our physical senses and our minds, what happens when we add our meta-physical senses to the mix?

Just a minute. I'll do the math.

Guess what? It adds up to our being super-sensitive! Except it makes no sense to add the soul's senses to the body's senses. Spirituality precedes physicality. Afterall, our souls have to wait for our bodies to be conceived so we can join them.

Can our souls sense without us? There is no sensing without us, but there is sensing within us. Whether our souls are sensing prior to incarnating, or while aligned with a physical body, or after departing, souls are living entities with their own ability to sense.

Looks like we have two sets of senses. Does everyone know about the second set?

7
Soulight

Soulight

Our minds are busy places! I soon discover how easily attention shifts. Having found the wheel, I steer my course, traveling back and forth through time like hands playing scales on a piano.

As I come to rest in the center of now, I feel myself expanding. Is my mind getting bigger too? Does that mean my head is swelling? How do I know my mind is inside my head? Am I a fancy suitcase with a mind packed inside it?

What if our minds coexist with our bodies, hovering in another dimension, moving when we move and stopping when we stop? Perhaps our minds don't take up any space. Space could be a relative concept, an assumption we have grown to rely on.

Maybe the ends of our bodies are only the ends we can see. There could be ends we can't see, energetic fields that reside outside our skin instead of in. What if those fields contain a record of our entire history and we carry our past with us?

This could explain how we sometimes know more about people than they tell us. We sense it. But which one of our senses can sense what someone has not told us?

Taking the Longing Out of Belonging

What about our souls? Do they live inside us like a pocket sewn inside a jacket? Or are our bodies on the inside and our souls on the outside, holding us around the waist like an illuminated belt?

Who said mental concepts can't change? Everything else does. Change is the one thing we can count on to stay the same.

And why can't we see souls? Is it because they exist outside the perceptual scope of our five senses?

"As you know, the universe is made of energy and energy vibrates," says the voice. "Sensing is the ability to detect those vibrations. Your eyes detect light vibrations; your ears detect sound vibrations; your nose detects scent vibrations; your mouth detects taste vibrations; your hands and other body parts detect pressure and temperature vibrations.

"In order to detect something, it has to be detectable. It has to be visible for you to see it, audible for you to hear it, and so on. Because your physical senses rely on measurable parameters."

Souls don't have a measurable presence! This is the reason we can't see them and why people question their existence. When we cannot see, or hear, or taste, or touch, or smell something, we assume it isn't there or it doesn't exist.

I know why we make that assumption. Our senses bring back information for our minds to process. When they come back empty handed, we have nothing to process. This leads us to conclude that nothing is there.

What if someone were calling to us from a distance? We might not be able to see them or hear them, but that wouldn't discount their existence. It simply demonstrates that our five senses have a limited range.

If we define reality based on what we sense and our five senses have a limited range, doesn't our thinking have a tendency to be limited?

"Fortunately, a tendency is not a certainty."

That is fortunate.

"Let's compare sensory perception to the reception you get on your television. Your body gets the basic channels, and your soul gets extended cable because it can pick up more signals."

Taking the Longing Out of Belonging

If my body's senses can pick up signals in the material realm, and my soul's senses can pick up signals in the non-material or spiritual realm, is there a link between the two?

"Yes, intuition is a bridge between realms. You are not confined to your five senses. You also have the ability to commune with your soul and sense what your soul senses."

Can I use my intuition to talk to my soul?

"You are doing it now. I'm the voice of your soul."

Some people claim to see deceased souls and talk to them. Will you explain that?

"They are communicating soul-to-soul. Sometimes, the soul's senses perceptually meld with the physical senses, which gives one the impression of having a visual and audible experience."

Are you saying that a person communicating with the deceased can see and hear souls just as well with their eyes closed and their ears covered, and they only think they are seeing and hearing in the traditional sense?

Soulight

"Look at the way we're conversing. I may use words, or sounds, or visions, or feelings, or tastes, or smells. None of these communications involve your external sensory organs."

I agree. I hear you, but there isn't any sound. Rather than hearing you with my outer ears, I am hearing you internally.

So, what I interpret as an inner voice, or inner vision, or inner guidance is you, my soul, talking to me. You sense the subtle values of life. My body senses the tangible values. And on occasion, my mind merges the two. I think I'm seeing, when I am really sensing what my soul is seeing.

"Exactly."

Is that what they call extrasensory perception?

"Extrasensory perception is not my favorite term. It implies an ability that is reserved for a select few. Everyone has a soul and is capable of sensing what their soul senses."

Maybe they should change the term to innersensory perception.

"Maybe they should."

I noticed you have been using the words "you" and "I" when you refer to us.

"Otherwise it might get confusing."

Are we a team?

"A team implies a group of separate individuals who share a common goal. You and I are not separate. I am your soul, and you are an extension of me. You are my current personality."

What do you mean?

"To have a fully integrated experience on Earth, the soul assumes a personality."

Like a role in a movie?

"Like a role where you relate to your character so completely – you believe it's who you are."

It's not who I am?

"It's who you have chosen to be in this lifetime."

Soulight

Are you saying my soul (you) chose this body and personality?

"Yes."

That sounds oddly familiar. Are there many appearances, and personalities, and life lessons for souls to choose from?

"Choice has the power to create an intention."

And I have the power to choose?

"You do."

If I was born with a mission, do the challenges I face have a higher purpose?

"Each challenge is an opportunity for growth."

Do you mean an opportunity to evolve?

"Yes, each challenge brings its own rewards."

Is there a way to see those rewards? Without seeing them, a number of us tend to take things at face value and find our challenges challenging.

"Meditating will help broaden your perspective and enhance your perception."

Can you sum up the benefits of meditation?

"Picture watering a garden every day and watching the flowers grow. When you meditate, you are the gardener and the garden. The flowers bloom in you."

Very poetic. What's the easiest way to keep in touch with you?

"Pay attention to what feels natural and what doesn't. That's a timeless code souls use to communicate. It has been around for eons and will help you stay on the most evolutionary path."

When something doesn't feel natural?

"Consider exploring other avenues until it does."

8
Immortality

Immortality

Does everybody have a soul, or does every soul have a body? What happens when this one runs out of fuel?

"Your soul and body share a life, like cyclists riding tandem. When your mortal body expires, your soul is freed to function on its own. Although dying is rarely well received among the living, it is a day of liberation for the soul."

Where will I go when my body retires?

"You'll go with your soul. Your human experience is only temporary."

Will I remember my life?

"Yes, and when you return to your heavenly abode and are reunited with souls you have known in past incarnations, you will remember those lives too. Your soul has lifetimes worth of memories."

Here on Earth, our memories prior to conception are practically vaulted shut like a door that only opens from one side. Unless we have a glimpse of our past lives and can see what nature's intentionally hidden from us.

Taking the Longing Out of Belonging

Some people who've witnessed their past lives report seeing friends and family in other bodies in their present lives.

"When you die, you will know you lived before. You just may not know it while you are still living – by earthly standards. Souls are as alive as humans and obviously a little better informed."

Are you saying my life will continue after the breath leaves my body?

"Of course, your life will continue. You will merely transition to a different style of functioning. You'll awaken from the dream of your earthly existence and reclaim your original form as a soul."

It must be when the human mind blankets the soul mind that we view our lives as ending.

"Must be."

What about now?

"Human life is precious. I suggest you honor it."

9
Glory

Glory

Late last night...in the dark...I found myself in the light. I was not female. I was not male. I had nothing to relate to. Now I can describe it. When it happened, there was not anything to describe until I heard a faint sound, a wrinkle on a blank canvas. The instant I recognized my name, I snapped back to a localized version of myself.

Except the snap was neither back nor forward. Being present doesn't have a direction.

To recapture that feeling, I sit comfortably to meditate. A thin veil of eyelid seals me in, as light streams unite my soul to this fine mass of energy we call a body. (Can anyone claim ownership for a privilege?)

When I settle down, I can feel my heart beating. Or is my heart breathing? Is love the breath of silence?

I am surfing now in the ocean of my mind, riding my thoughts to the shoreline. Consciousness greets them the way the eye catches sight of a shooting star as it whips by, then sizzles out of sight.

Something is happening! I feel like a snake shedding its skin, like water being purified. I am detoxifying, realigning, redefining.

Taking the Longing Out of Belonging

Yesterday's meanings lose their meaning, diffusing the embers of what was. All that remains is the liquid simplicity of what is.

I awake and find myself exactly where I am. In that instant, I realize it is where I have always been.

Awash in humility, gravity recedes. I am weightless in an expanse with no beginning or end, where time is timeless and points are pointless. At the inception of all things beautiful we call life. The holy crevice – where change ascends from the changeless and diversity resides before diverging. Here, creativity meets her muse.

I am in a free-fall. Adrift in a soundless sea. Going deeper and deeper within. Beyond perception and inception, the only thing that exists is existence.

My desires eclipsed, I stand silent witness to glory. To freedom. To wanting nothing and having everything. Lifetimes of trying extinguished by a solitary moment of pure presence.

Full to overflowing, confidence wraps itself around my shoulders. Yielding to innocence, the universe reveals eternity without blinking.

Glory

Divinely sanctioned, my singularity falters. When I feel, the world feels with me. When I think, the world thinks with me. When I move, the world moves with me.

Which feelings are mine? Which thoughts are mine? Which movements are mine? None of it belongs to me. Yet, all of it belongs to me the way moisture belongs to rain and heat to fire.

What an idea! It's the icing on the cake of ideas. We are not solitary waves separate from that which is waveless. We are dancers in a divine play, players in a divine dance. Living exponents of the shapeless shaping, the unexpressed expressing itself through this vehicle I call *myself* and you call *yourself*.

When the truth is, each of us personifies something selfless. A super-conductible, quantum-mechanical spring of untold proportions pregnant with possibilities.

I am rejuvenated, internally rocked with peaceful elation and invigorating delight. Tears fill my eyes as I realize the magnitude of raw energy I am privy to, the incomprehensible gift of co-creating with such authority.

Taking the Longing Out of Belonging

The mundane joins the extraordinary, as I open my eyes and see energy pretending to be matter. As soon as the thought forms, mental bondage fades out of influence. Energy does not pretend. The seer, not the seen, brings definition.

Was the world bathed in light while I meditated, or am I seeing clearly for the first time?

10
Belonging

Belonging

I see an all-pervading inner glow in everyone. The same source pulses in each of us.

Physicists call it the unified field. Spiritualists call it home. With this blessed sense of home lively in my awareness, I finally feel content. For years, I sought to find fulfillment. Now it has found me.

Recognition dawns. Belonging isn't limited to membership, or ownership, or categorical groupings that include some and exclude others. The real meaning of belonging does not divide. It unites the way all hearts beat as one.

Who is there to greet newly manifest impulses? The answer is belonging.

Present at every birth, she witnesses purity becoming pure, love becoming loving, inspiration becoming inspiring. Belonging is the divine maternal instinct spread like jam throughout a universe of diversity, and we are her children.

We are souls clothed in human forms. Our spiritual bodies and physical bodies engage in an on-going duet, as mysticism taps her feet to keep the pace, the rhythm, the motionless in motion.

Taking the Longing Out of Belonging

I belong to you and you belong to me. We belong to spirit and spirit belongs to us. We belong to humanity and humanity belongs to us. We are all family in the eyes of the infinite.

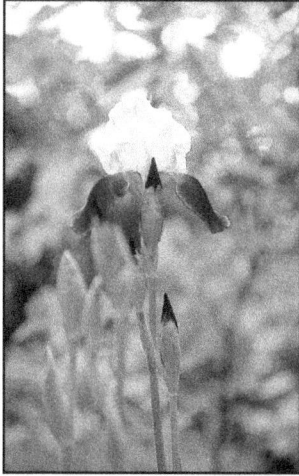

11
Divine Inheritance

Divine Inheritance

If you are reading this book or listening to these words, neither event is random. There are signs teachers agree to prior to incarnating. Vibrational triggers that greet us like old friends, sending wake-up calls to our knowing place.

If compassion speaks louder to you than judgment; if you question the surface values of life and feel pulled to know what lies beyond; if your heart demands that you reach out to others; if your desire to make a difference in this world is too big to live small, consider your light lit.

Your internal compass led you to the altar floating in your heart. On it is a mirror reflecting your hopes and dreams surrounded by a flurry of excitement, as cosmic forces gather to celebrate your divine inheritance.

Who is divine? You are the promise to behold.

Remember when you had roll call in grade school? It appears your role has been called, affirming your membership in an anointed support group united by intent. Together, we hold an agreement in our collective palms to lead by example. (To lead is to be led by one's own commitment to truth.)

Taking the Longing Out of Belonging

We lead by example the same way a teacher teaches by example: To teach others to trust, trust yourself. To teach others to value, value yourself. To teach others to enjoy, enjoy yourself. To teach others to accept, accept yourself. To teach others to forgive, forgive yourself. To teach others to respect, respect yourself. To teach others to nurture, nurture yourself. To teach others to lead, embody what you teach.

This agreement is actualized by being the luminary you are. Ablaze from within and beaming outward so others can see their celebrity in your radiance. As you ride – paraglide – the winds of change blowing on the surface of that which is non-changing.

So begins the journey for those willing to surrender the path for the goal, the hunt for the treasure, the finite for the infinite. For when we align with the power within us, life responds in kind.

Invoking the chant to end our search and begin our solace, belonging whispers a reminder: To love from the soul of love, as the sun shines from the sun of love. As the moon beams from the moon of love, share your majesty.

To teach others to love, love yourself. To teach others to honor, honor yourself. To teach others to cherish, cherish yourself. To teach others to love, love yourself.

Share Your Majesty

About the Author

I've been practicing the Transcendental Meditation technique for close to four decades, meditating once in the morning upon rising and again in the late afternoon or early evening. When I first began, I meditated twenty minutes twice a day. Soon after, I learned the TM-Sidhi Program, which requires a longer commitment twice daily.

When asked how I find the time, I repeat something I heard Maharishi Mahesh Yogi, the founder of the Transcendental Meditation movement, say: "Think of your program as your office hours and everything in between as recreation."

I took those words to heart and have abided by them ever since, enjoying many benefits from my regular meditation practice: Even in the midst of dynamic activity, silence and calm permeate my day. I feel rooted from within and connected to all of life. My creativity flows like a fountain. Best of all, I have an ongoing feeling of optimism. Sometimes, happiness and gratitude bubble up inside me for no apparent reason.

Kira Rosner

Why is this relevant? Because I am not dependent on outside circumstances to dictate how I feel. I'm sensitive to what takes place around me, but I rely more on an inner sense of stability than an outer.

We're all born with the potential to commune with our divine nature. Taking an inward dive on a daily basis has helped me cultivate that ability. For this, I am deeply grateful to Maharishi Mahesh Yogi, whose tireless commitment to end suffering has improved the lives of millions of people around the world.

I give thanks every day for this simple, yet profound technique. It is like having the key to my very own kingdom, except it is not mine to own. It's ours.

Shall we put our palms together and praise this life force we've been entrusted with? What we do with it is up to us.

About the Artist

"My art is about the beauty of the natural world –
the delicacy of a flower's bloom, a seashell, a patch
of sunlight on sparkling waters. Beauty that is seen
and unseen, but felt in the depths of the heart."

Terrence Kennedy

Terrence Kennedy

For Terrence Kennedy, art is a bridge between his artistic and spiritual interests, allowing him to share his most heartfelt and cherished visions. In this way, Terrence hopes some essence of celestial beauty will emerge from each piece and be enlivened within the heart of every viewer.

All the images in this book are either oil paintings or watercolors with the exception of "David's Iris." This image represents Terrence's recent body of work, demonstrating his love for both painting and photography.

By applying layers of translucent glazes and drops of pure color to the surface of his black and white photographs, he extracts luminous forms. Created on archival paper with pigment based inks which insure stability and permanence, Terrence's refined works of art will be cherished for generations.

www.Higher-Essence.com

Also by Kira Rosner

When Souls Take Flight: Coping with Grief

"Your soul is lit from within, and that light is a spark of divinity shining through you."

Kira Rosner, *When Souls Take Flight*

This heartfelt book explains what happens when we die, shining light on a subject that is often equated with darkness. It offers comforting advice for anyone who is grieving, caring for a loved one in their final days, or facing their own terminal illness.

If you have lost someone you love, or are about to, this book was written for you.

– Available At Your Favorite Bookstores –
Online & Off

Print: ISBN 978-0-9679978-2-7
eBook: ISBN 978-0-9679978-1-0

www.KiraRosner.com

Books by Kira Rosner

The Power of Being Human
Taking the Longing Out of Belonging
When Souls Take Flight: Coping with Grief

*These books share a common thread
and may contain similar excerpts.

www.KiraRosner.com

www.ingramcontent.com/pod-product-compliance
Lightning Source LLC
Chambersburg PA
CBHW031329040426
42443CB00005B/270